Foundation: A Blueprint For Business Success

NEIL HOWE

The Authority Architect

Foundation:
A Blueprint For Business Success

© 2015

Neil Howe
A.C.E. Marketing
Atlanta, Georgia

ISBN: **0692494855**
ISBN13: **978-0692494851**

Edited by Kristina Jacobs, PhD

Testimonials

"Neil Howe is a true authority powerhouse. Whether you want your book to be an Amazon best-seller, want your press releases to be picked up all over the world or want television and radio producers blowing up your phone, you need Neil's services. Thanks, Neil, for the success you've helped me achieve!" – **Sandy Weaver Carman, Voicework On Demand, Inc.**

"I became a client of Neil's last year and have been very impressed with his savvy ability in regards to Authority Marketing. Neil has been amazingly helpful to my business and personal reputation in regards to articles and videos that have gotten several mentions in online publications like ABC, NBC, Fox and more. Also he has been vital in increasing my presence as an authority figure in the Digital/Mobile and Social Media Strategy niche. My business has been in existence for 6 years and Neil and his agency have done more in regards to marketing and increasing my personal presence as an expert in my field than anything I have previously attempted. Neil is very effective in developing a marketing/authority strategy for you and your business that is above and beyond anyone else out there. I highly recommend Neil and Authority Marketing for those individuals

and entrepreneurs who have worked hard and created a solid business and are ready for the next level." – Les Adkins, CEO Orange SMS

"If you do not 'know' Neil Howe and his expertise in positioning your greatness, then you are losing value, time and ground of being known as THE expert in your field. You will 'like' Neil and the services he provides to bring you and your business to Celebrity Authority status. 'Trust' me when I tell you the Buzz and Benefits you will receive from Neil's genius are worth every dollar spent to elevate your image. Our project with Neil resulted in reaching Amazon #1 Best Seller for our book, Happiness Recipe: Whippin' up wit, wisdom and wonderful food! Neil Howe takes the time-tested sales formula, "know, like, trust," to new heights as he elevates you and your business to celebrity status. I cannot recommend more highly the genius and expertise of Neil Howe." – June Cline, CSP

---œœo---

Table of Contents

---œœo---

INTRODUCTION

Hi, my name is Neil Howe and over the last 10 years I have been helping local business owners generate more leads and profits through online advertising and SEO.
As a local business owner myself, I know the problems local business owners face when it comes to marketing and working their business. I have experienced the highs of getting clients steady new customers by being on the first page of Google as well as feeling the sting of the Google Slap that hurt so many businesses that relied on Google too much as their sole source of new customers.

My passion is to help local business owners and entrepreneurs develop a strong foundation to their business by positioning them as the authority in their market, so they can attract only the best, highest paying customers, clients or patients that they want to work with, without ever having to be at the mercy of Google or any other single media for survival.

This new method I've been teaching for the past couple of years called "Authority Marketing" is so much more powerful than anything I have taught in the last 10 years and has had the biggest impact on my own and my clients' businesses, transforming them into nationally recognized powerhouses in their industries.

CHAPTER ONE

The first thing that a local business owner should do if they're interested in authority marketing is define their **globally desired position**, which means thinking about what position they actually want to take in their marketplace.

When we're thinking about that, it's like how they actually want to be perceived by their potential customers, clients or patients, so what they are actually thinking about before even engaging with that person or business. What is their perception of that company?

What's Your Globally Desired Position?

It's very important for a local business owner to decide exactly what it is that they want to be in their market, and then you want to figure out from there how you're going to get the most money from your community while delivering your service with goodwill. Once you have that established, then you can build that perfect message so that you're attracting your ideal clientele, those people that you really want to be working with.

A good place to start is uncovering what you and your business do best. Something that you enjoy doing, which you have a passion for, is going to keep you motivated in the business, but you really have to do two things. You need to know how to do something that fulfills a "white hot" desire or provides an important solution for people with the ability to compensate you for it. There is no point in getting into a market if there's no money in it.

The SPAN Method

Obviously, you need to know how to do that, and you also need to be able to package it, and market, and be able to sell that thing. A good test for that is the SPAN method. **SPAN stands for Specific, Pain, Attainable, and Numbers.** Specific comes down to a micro-specialization, which means you don't want to be the "Jack of all trades" and the "master of none" because you don't want to be that person that does everything for everybody. You want to break it down to what you're really good at and what you specialize in, what we call "micro-specialization."

To give you an example, in the financial industry you've got somebody like Dave Ramsey, who teaches finance. The financial industry is a huge industry. You've got trading and stocks, but his specialization or his micro-specialization is getting people out of debt. That's the only thing that he concentrates on - he teaches people how to get out of debt and how to cut up those credit cards.

That's being very specific in the market, and that's setting that desired position of what he really wants to be known for. So, for an example, in local business you may be a lawyer who could cover any number of litigations, but if you truly want to be known, you need to choose what you do best. It may be injury, divorce, malpractice, family, or real estate, but, you really have to choose your focus.

The second part of the SPAN is the "P," which is the pain. Are you solving a problem that really needs to be solved? Like I said before, there's either got to be a "white-hot" desire that people really want this product or service or you're solving a problem that really needs to be solved. If there isn't some kind of pain there in the market then you're probably not going to get a great response from it.

The "A" in SPAN is for attainable, which means are you really in a position once you've decided that this is what you are going to do and you're passionate about it, are you really in a position to help people to solve that problem? It's fine getting into a market and saying, "Well, there's really a need here for this," but if you're not in a position to solve that problem and you give a bad customer experience that's bad goodwill for your business. That's not something that you want to do. You're not going to be in business long if you're not really solving people's problems properly. So, you have to be qualified to solve the problem professionally.

The final letter in SPAN is "N" for numbers. Are there enough people or enough of a market to make it worthwhile? If it's something like underwater basket weaving there probably isn't a great market for that, so you really need to look at the numbers. A great way you can do that is just by going to Google and typing it in, and seeing if there are people searching for that, having a look at the actual search volume that Google comes back with. Another good way to test is, especially in local markets, is if there's any advertising from Google down the side. That shows that it's a market that people are willing to spend money in.

Remember, do the SPAN test to discover what it is that you do best as a company, this is part of defining your **globally desired position**.

What Do You Stand For?

You also want to be sure you stand for something. You want to be known as a certain kind of company. To give you an example of what you should stand for, my wife has a cleaning company here in Atlanta and it's a non-toxic cleaning company, so that is what we want to be known for is being a non-toxic cleaning company. If you know anything about the chemicals in household cleaners, they are extremely toxic to your health and cause all sorts of problems.

There's a massive market out there right now for green cleaning but, again, we have our own views on that, to where green cleaning isn't really non-toxic, so we really wanted to stand out as that non-toxic cleaning company, which means this is a safe cleaning service. Our clientele proves that as we have many pregnant mothers, or mothers of toddlers, or people with skin irritations. Those people are seeking out that specific non-toxic cleaning, which is what we want to stand for.

By doing that we are attracting the people that understand our business, understand what we offer; therefore, it becomes a lot easier to work with and be appreciated by those kinds of people.

When you gather customers or clients like that they tend to stay a lot longer and they are a lot more loyal to you and your business because you share that common bond. You have something in common. People want to engage with like-minded people.

My wife will go to somebody's house and she can stand and talk to them for 20, 30 minutes about the new products, and that's developing relationships in business. You're building that tribe of like-minded people, and they're going to be a lot more loyal with you and stay on for a greater time and be more vocal about recommending you and giving referrals to other people and reviews online. You want to have something in common with people so that they can talk passionately about it.

What Do You Stand Against?

Those would be our ideal customers, and those are the people that we want to attract, but at the same time you also want to share what you stand against. Like I said with our example of the cleaning, the chemical toxins in cleaners are something that we stand against. There's a million and one cleaning companies out there that use the cheapest solutions that they can possibly get just so that their saving money. It's incredibly harmful to not only the cleaners who are using it every day but they're going into their customer's homes and they're spreading all those chemicals all over the place.

From that standpoint as well we want to share with our market that we stand against that; that's not something that we do, so if somebody comes and says, "Can you just use bleach on that," they should know, "No, we don't, because it's a toxic chemical." We want to stand against a lack of quality also, and by using some of the top-of-the-line non-toxic cleaners we establish a better level of quality than the other companies out there that are using cheaper solutions. Of course everything comes down to customer service as well. The more goodwill you provide in your community the more chance you're going to have of referrals and gaining a long-term customer base.

The first thing that a local business owners who are interested in establishing themselves as an authority should do is truly define for themselves and their business what their globally desired position is, and to do that, you should uncover what your business does best, what you stand for, and what you stand against.

Then it is important to do the SPAN test, utilizing this idea of uncovering your micro-specialization. Remember, it's "specific." What pain are you solving? Is it attainable? Are you qualified to solve that problem, and are there enough people to really have that make sense so that there's a market for the solution that you want to offer?

There are many people that get into business just because they have a passion around something, and then they spend all their time and their money trying to grow that business only to discover that nobody else really has that same passion as they do, and the money is not there for them to make a living.

In the end, you could be very passionate about the business and solving a problem but, there has to be enough of a need for your solution that it's going to be able to make the amount of money and support the size business that you want to create. This is why it is so important for local business owners to attract their ideal clients.

CHAPTER TWO

The first thing, you need to do to attract your ideal client is to create a clear message that speaks to specific problems that your ideal customers, clients or patients are going to be seeking out. Keep in mind, figuring out who your ideal client is should take into account your globally desired position within the market.

How To Attract Your Ideal Clients

You definitely want to speak to specific problems, and a great way to do that is with what we call "one problem, one solution marketing." For example, when searching for a Chiropractor, if the problem that somebody is having is that they have foot pain, they're going to be searching for a Chiropractor that deals with foot pain. That's a very specific search.

If you can address that problem then you're in a greater position to be able to help, so talking about Dave Ramsey again, as we gave that example earlier on, his one problem is how to get out of credit card debt. That's what he focuses on, and all his solutions solve that problem. There might be a bunch of questions that people have about how to get out of credit card debt, but his solutions are all revolved around getting out of credit card debt, so he becomes known for that specific problem within the financial market.

Another person within the financial market as well is Suze Orman. On her show people call in and explain on the show the position that they're in with their finances, and she is all about giving the advice of can the person afford to buy this or do they need to save their money? "Can I afford to buy a boat right now?" and she's going to say, "No. That's not a wise investment. You need to do this. Do this. Do that." That's her niche as well.

Somebody else within the fitness niche, Richard Simmons, who's been around for decades, his market is the severely overweight. That market is growing in America. The severely overweight is his market, so he's not really talking about how to get on the bench press and lift the most weight. He's not talking about buffing up and having that toned physique. He's helping people live their lives or get to a manageable position by losing the weight, to where they can actually function. That's his specific market that he is known for.

Create A Clear Message

You have to have a clear message so people know what you're all about, so when they come to your website, or in the local market when they come to your place of business they should know right away what you do and how you're going to be able to help them. A good way to design that is by developing a strong USP, which is a unique selling proposition.

The best and the most famous one out there that people know is from Domino's Pizza. Their USP is, "Fresh, hot pizza delivered to your door in 30 minutes or less, or it's free." That USP right there built their whole brand. It told people exactly what they were getting: fresh, hot pizza. It didn't necessarily say anything about the quality, or the taste, or anything else. It was just fresh, hot pizza, and it was going to be delivered to your door in 30 minutes or less, or it's free. That was their guarantee.

That's a very specific USP. If people are hungry and they want food right now or within 30 minutes they know that they can call up Domino's and get fresh, hot pizza delivered, and if they don't fulfill their promise then it's going to be free. That built them into a multi-million dollar business that's still one of the biggest and best-known pizza companies in the whole world right now.

Build Your Brand Around Your Message

There are other things that the businesses can do to clarify their message, to create their brand, and attract their ideal clients. When it comes to actually attracting the clients, you want to be seeking them out when they are looking for solutions to problems. A great way to do that is by answering specific questions that your potential customers might have. Any business owner or secretary, or somebody that answers the phone, knows what the most frequently asked questions are. If you could design some content, whether it's a video or even just a blog post or something on your website around those most frequently asked questions, and you can answer them, then you're giving your customers the answers to the questions when they're looking for it.

That puts you in a position of authority when you become a teacher or an educator like that.

At the same time there's those frequently asked questions, but from a professional standpoint you might know what we call the "should-ask" questions. They might be asking these 10 most frequently asked questions, but here's the 10 questions that they should be asking, and maybe these are the questions that they get to a little bit later on once they really figured out what it is that they want.

As far as attracting people to you and developing your brand around that certain message, if you can answer 10 frequently asked questions and 10 should-ask questions, if you can develop content around all that and get it out on blogs, and videos, and social media, and articles, interviews, audios, if you can get it out on all these different places then whenever people within your market are searching for answers, you can direct them back to your website. Once they're on your website and you've provided good quality information and goodwill by answering their questions, you become that automatic choice or their go-to person in their market to solve the problems that they have. That's a great way to drive qualified traffic.

This is how the local businesses are discovering that these are their ideal clients, because they're providing the content when the person who needs the solution is actually looking for it. They've got it fresh in their mind, "I'm going to do something about this," and then their really just vetting the company, "Do I want to work with them or not?" You touched on making this content and sharing it through blogs, videos, social media, and all over the place, and I know that that comes back to this idea that we want to talk about of making yourself so that people understand that you're the authority in your industry.

Be Seen As An Authority

One of the things to be seen as an authority is to just distribute that content on authority domains. Now, authority domains in Google's eyes are the domains that have the most trusted authority. Some of those examples are sites like YouTube and Twitter and Facebook and LinkedIn. These are all high-value sites to Google. They rank extremely high on the search engines, so whenever you're creating content it's great to put it on your own website, but it's also more beneficial to probably to put it out on all these different authority domains because it's a lot easier for people to find that on YouTube and other social sites as that is where they are hanging out.

A YouTube video is going to rank probably a lot higher than a personal business website, so if you really want people to find you, you need to get your content out on some of those authority sites. There's also local directories like Yellow Pages, Yelp,

Thumbtack, HomeAdvisor. These sites are all classified as authority sites in Google's eyes, so to get your business listed in those kind of sites is really important too.

Then, of course, we have the massive media authority sites like ABC and CBS, NBC, FOX, CNN, USA Today, as well as some of the top newspapers that have their online publications as well, like The Boston Globe and the Miami Herald. These are all authority sites as well, which not only helps you be found on their sites, but they also give you that third-party authority. The authority that these media sites have, they're basically lending that authority to you, and to your business, and what you're saying just by featuring you on their site. That can be really, really powerful.

People trust ABC or CBS or NBC, and you're trying to help them trust your business. It's a transfer of that trust and authority that that media company has built over the decades. ABC, CBS, NBC, FOX, CNN, these are all well-known, trusted authority networks, and if you can be positioned on those networks, then, yes, that trust and authority is transferred over to you because they wouldn't be covering you if you weren't somebody influential and important. So, if you are a doctor that helps people lose weight through surgery and you are featured on one of these publications it is like a personal endorsement from that media site to say that you are the best in the area at what you do and that is why they covered your story.

By being the authority as well you also want to show up everywhere, and this is what helps you show up as well. If you have a link on YouTube and Twitter and Facebook and some of these newspapers and media places, and somebody is searching for a specific problem, that one problem, one solution, if the results come back from Google or Yahoo or whatever they search, your company is coming up in 6, 7, 8 of the 10 results on Google, then instantly you're going to be the go-to company, so getting your message out across all these authority domains is extremely important.

When you're seen everywhere familiarity provides trust. You're not giving a sales message out on all of these sites; you're showing that you're an expert, and that you want to be able to help the people who have these problems, and that you're there, you're advocating for their success. That draws people to you.

Really all of this is predicated on how many more people are using the Internet to look for businesses, or their smartphone or tablet, though this is just in addition to face-to-face traditional marketing and business methods.

Face to face, especially in local business, is still extremely important. Referral business has been the top kind of business for many years, but what we find now is people are so connected to the Internet that, yes, they're going on there, and they're searching. Even when they do get a referral from somebody that is face to face, the first thing that they do is they go online to look for reviews and testimonials and recommendations about that business. The Internet is the first place that potential customers are going to find out new information about local businesses.

Know Your Value

A common mistake that businesses who are trying to attract their ideal clients make when they're first starting out is to compete on price. That's never something that you want to get involved in, trying to be the low-price leader, unless you're a Walmart. There aren't too many other companies out there that can compete with Walmart, being the low-price leader. They are a massive, massive company that has huge branding, and the only way that Walmart works is because they have such narrow margins.

In fact, to tell you a story, I just read the other day about the pressure that Walmart has been under to raise their minimum wage to $15. They've done that in certain places, but what they've done, because they have such power, they went to all their distributors and said, "You need to cut your prices by 10% so that we can afford to pay our workers that $15 minimum wage," because if they had to raise their prices their business model wouldn't work anymore. You never want to be that person that is the lowest price person in your market.

You really have to know your value. In order to do that you really need to define who you want to work with. Do you want to work with people who are struggling to pay you? That's not going to lead to much success. You don't want to get on the phone and start haggling with people about cut-rate jobs. I mentioned my wife's business before as well. As a cleaning business you're one of many in that market, and you want to be able to stand out from the competition a lot more, but as one of many, people would call up and say they always wanted a better price.

We don't want to be in a position of haggling. There's a bunch of companies out there that are going to do it for cheaper than we do, but talking about that authority with the ABC, NBC, CBS, once we put those logos on our website, people stopped doing that. They stopped asking for price breaks because they saw our positioning was of the upper lever and they understood that they were going to have to pay a little bit more.

Anyway, you never want to take cut-rate jobs. You need to expect to be paid top dollar for providing quality service. You never want to get into price wars and haggling, and you don't ever want to complete on price because it's not really the deciding factor for most people; it only accounts for about 10% of the buying decision. That's one of the main things that people make the mistake of when they're getting into business. They're always trying to compete on price. They should really be establishing their position so that they don't have to compete on price with everybody else.

CHAPTER THREE

Authority positioning is what you want people to see you as before they actually do business with you. If the message when they get to your website or come into your store is not clear, then they don't know what they're getting involved with and are going to try and control the outcome themselves.

What is Authority Positioning?

If your message is strong and you're featured as an authority, on all these media channels, and you've written books on this and that, then people immediately understand that they're dealing with the best and one of the top people in the market. That's what authority positioning is, and you want to be positioned as the best in your local market.

Positioning YOU As The Authority

It doesn't matter really where you start. General Sun Tzu from his book The Art of War says, "When you're small you need to appear big." That's where you need to start out. It's that appearance that you want to give to people who are searching for you, that you are the top and you are the authority. Like I said, using those media sites, especially the ABC, the NBC, that lends tremendous trust and credibility when you put your content out there. That transfer of authority from them to you really goes a long way to establish your positioning and your authority.

None of this is about calling yourself the expert either. You are allowing other people to call you the expert which is completely different than your competition. They all have the same vanilla message of being in business for x amount of years and have quality service...its all the same, boring and bland. It's very easy to stand out with a little authority.

When you're positioned as authority by other people and you have other people talking about you in a positive manner, it's going to give you a lot more confidence in yourself. That is one of the most important things in any business is to have that confidence in yourself because people know right away who they're dealing with, and if you're not sure of yourself people will see that very quickly and they'll be hesitant about doing business with you.

I had a client who's a real estate agent, and we featured her on ABC and NBC and CBS, and she put those logos on her website, and she just said it gave her so much more confidence that she went to meetings knowing that she was in a position of power. She was able to help people, and she was able to increase her sales by just that. It was just that air of confidence about her that people were drawn to, and because of the confidence, it led to an increase in her sales.

You've got to have that confidence in yourself that also gives you belief about selling your product and service, and people who are passionate about selling the product and service that comes through in a sales presentation and attracts people to you as well. Those are the two major things that really help the business owner, what the authority positioning does for the business owner, and it also gives you more value in the eyes of your customers. By doing all these things it helps you increase the prices for your services because like we said, when you've established that position people almost expect to pay more and are willing to pay more for your services. By doing this it really helps you increase your price.

How Does Authority Positioning Help ME?

Authority positioning goes hand in hand with what it does for the business owner himself. The clients see the confidence that you have and it gives them the faith in you that you're going to be able to solve their problems and help them get to their desired outcome. It also gives them trust in you, especially if you're featured on these major networks. That transference of trust: If the major networks are covering you then you must be somebody who is trustworthy and is going to follow through and has given quality service before; otherwise you wouldn't have been featured.

It sets the expectations before your customers even deal with you, which we call "pre-framing." They have an idea in their heads what the experience is going to be and what they're going to expect before they even deal with you.

How Does Authority Positioning Help Clients?

They have that faith in you. They have that trust in you. They have an idea that they're going to get quality service from you, and also that they're going to maybe have to pay a little bit more, but people are inclined to pay more for better service, and also really attracts your ideal customers to you.

What Authority Positioning Is NOT

A word of warning for businesses just beginning to think about authority positioning, it's not about calling yourself the expert, and it's not about a sales message all the time. You want to be that educator and advocate for the success of your clientele, and that's the position that you want to take. It's not about calling yourself the expert. It's about helping people and being viewed as the expert by other people, especially when third parties are telling other people that you are the expert. That gives you all the credibility, so much more than calling yourself the expert could ever do.

The other thing about being the authority is people think that they have to know everything. They're not the top in their industry, and they have to know everything before they can be called the authority. That's not what this is about at all. It's not about being the absolute best at what you do. There may be many people qualified to do what you do, but only a few are going to stand out as the authority. There are 13 dentists for every Starbucks in America, which is a lot of competition, but the authority is going to be able to draw a bigger clientele from a wider area than the other strugglers. This doesn't just happen. It's not about waiting years to be anointed the authority by the authority gods or whoever is supposed to be doing this anointing. People shouldn't be waiting around to be classified as an authority. They have to actually go out there and claim it.

CHAPTER FOUR

So, what is an authority really? It's somebody who's willing and able to help other people solve problems or achieve an outcome, and letting them know that they're available to help.

What Makes Me An Authority?

That's all it really is. If you can help me get to my solution quicker or solve my problem faster then, to me, you're an authority, and that's really the only position that you have to be in to call yourself an expert and position yourself as an authority.

Knowing More Than Your Prospects

A lot of business owners may be hesitant to call themselves an authority. They could be sitting there asking, "What makes me an authority?" It's about knowing more than your prospects. If you have a plumbing issue, who is more superior? Is it a plumber, or is it the CEO of a massive company that might make a million dollars, or is it the plumber that makes $70,000? Who's the authority in that situation? Obviously it's the plumber.

To give you a personal example, the other day I had to call a plumber to the house to fix my dishwasher that stopped working. The water wasn't getting in there and I couldn't wash the dishes, so I'm washing the dishes in the sink, and doing it all by hand, and drying them, and putting them away. It's a pain. I'm thinking there's some technical problem with my dishwasher. I don't know how to fix it. I needed an authority, somebody that knows a little bit more than me, to come in here and solve my problem. A little embarrassing is that the guy came in, fiddled around for two seconds and found out that my little plug was filled up with dishwashing soap. He cleaned it out and everything started working right away.

But it cost me $80 for somebody to come out just to do that, but the fact is, his knowledge was more superior to mine for that circumstance, and if I hadn't called him out I would still be taking all my time washing those dishes by hand. That makes somebody an authority, just because they know a little bit more than I do about that specific problem, and of course you've got to be willing and able to help. Coming out to the house and being able to do what he did, he was willing and able to help, and that's what we're looking for.

I think a problem in the local market and every market is almost competent has become the new good, so if you are good at what you do and you provide a quality product or service, then people will flock to you. Almost competent is what this world has come to, so if you really know how to provide that quality service, people are going to seek you out.

Being Seen As An Educator

When you think about educators you think about teachers or professors. Immediately when you think about that you put them in a position of authority because they're perceived to know way more than you do. They've put in all the studying and the time to get to the position that they are, so when you're a teacher or an educator you immediately have that position of authority. That's what I was talking about earlier, just answering those frequently asked questions or those should-ask questions. If you can do that and you're seen as a teacher, you're immediately thought of as an authority, and people want to do business with authority.

If you can get that information out through seminars or interviews or webinars or classes or books especially, if you wrote the book on something then you're immediately a class above anybody else out there, so it's really important to get that information out there that is in your head to people and to be seen as that teacher and educator. It also puts you in that position of trust because people trust teachers and educators to give quality information, and they're certainly more willing listen to your advice when you are talking. They're going to take that advice and use it, so if you give a recommendation to them that this is what they need to do, because you're that teacher or that educator, they're going to take that advice to heart. If it's something that they don't think they can do themselves you become the obvious choice for them when it's time to make decisions to solve that problem.

A lot of people think that they don't want to give away their secrets or their best information, but what I find and what most other successful people find is that by giving away some of their best information and their best stuff it actually just draws people to them, because even when people know how to do some things it's either a hassle or they're just not confident in getting their desired outcome, so they will go back to you for the "done for you" solution.

Be Willing And Able To Help – Advocate

Being willing to help going to help you be an authority in someone's eyes. If you know anything about Richard Simmons, he is deeply involved, very attached to what he does, and people can see that. They can see that he really cares about his clientele and getting the best for them, and that draws people to you. When you become an advocate for the success of your customers, your clients, or patients, that's something that people really want, and when they see that, they want to do business with you.

"Almost Competent" has become the new good, and people are really looking for old-time values, they want to be appreciated. They want to be understood. They want to be cared for, and that's what they're looking for. They're looking for that relationship with somebody to do business with, and if you can combine that with up-to-date technology, which they also expect, you're really going attract a lot of people to you.

People are desperate to be treated with respect and dignity. If you can do that and you can show that to your customers, first of all, they're going to love you. They're going to be loyal to you, and to you company, and to your brand. They're going to talk about you, and of course they're also going to give you a lot more referrals because of the great experience with you.

Being Recognized By Others

Authorities are recognized in the media because the media wants to talk about people who are important in their eyes all the time, so you've got to be coming out with new content and getting it out on these local channels, national channels. Of course if you're positioned on national channels like ABC, NBC, CBS that gives you the authority across the board, but getting positioned on the local channels as well is just the same. You get that specific geographical authority from that market too. So, if you are featured on CBS Atlanta, it is really relevant to people in that Atlanta market.

It's very important to get out there and be interviewed as an expert by being a guest on podcast or radio or maybe local TV stations about what you do, what difference you make in the community, and telling people what you stand for, and advocating and helping and educating. Those are the kinds of things that, the TV and the radio stations are looking for to give that quality information to their audience.

CHAPTER FIVE

I'll give you an example. Say I was the local pest control company and I'm trying to expand my customer base from my local small town to some of the larger towns surrounding me. The local pest control company can use authority positioning to find their ideal clients.

How Do I Stand Out From The Competition?

When you're positioned as somebody in the media, and when you're positioned as an authority, people see that right away, so if you've already been talked about by some of these other media places, you can go to the next town and you can share with them where you've been featured before. You might get on the local TV station as a new business coming to town that offers a specific service. You might get on different radio shows that have a local audience that you're looking for, so that you can get your message again, get that message out to the local clientele. It's very important even when you're moving into a new market to move in as the authority, and by talking to as many people as possible within that area is the best way to do that.

Become A Resource

By getting on these radio shows that have hundreds of listeners, or local media channels and sharing that in the local market is one of the best ways to get your word out. A great way to do that, to get on a radio show or TV is by writing a book about what you do, because authorities write books and that's a great way to get on the radio is to talk about your book.

It's also great when you're on the radio if you can be announced as a bestseller. It's a great introduction if you're onstage or at an event or anything is to be announced as a bestseller. That immediately puts you in a position of authority and gets you that recognition in a new local market.

For example, the pest control company owner might write a book talking about all of the different pests local to that area and how to treat them.

Because you've written that book and people who are searching out pest control see that, you're immediately positioned as the authority. Those are the trust factors that prospects look for and they want to do business with businesses with that kind of credibility. The great thing about this, of course, is all this can be manufactured out of thin air.

CHAPTER SIX

You look at people who are authorities in the media right now, Bruce Jenner and the Kardashians and Paris Hilton. These people get recognized in the media all the time, and the reason they get recognized is because they're always putting themselves out there for something. They haven't done anything. They don't really have much substance, but they're always putting themselves out there to be featured in some way.

Be Seen Everywhere

They're going to the media and saying, "I want to be relevant. I want to be talked about. Here I am. I've done something. Cover it." You really need to be going to these radio stations and TVs and sharing with them. What you're doing is trying to stay relevant because if you wait to be anointed, for somebody to find out about you, you're going to be waiting for an awful long time.

Local businesses need to start being proactive and letting their different media outlets know whenever anything has happened in their business that might be newsworthy so that they can start getting the recognition they deserve

It can even start out with just social media, by always putting something out on social media, whether it's just an answer to a question. There is also something called "News Jacking," which is looking at relevant stories in the news media and finding a connection to it and your local business.

For example, there was a really bad car accident recently that went viral of a police officer trying to comfort a child who was ejected from an SUV by singing her a lullaby. If you look at the story there are many angles for local businesses to take advantage of the massive media coverage it got. The father of 5 died without any life insurance. The kids were improperly restrained. The tire blew out. The SUV rolled 3 times. Now think of all the local businesses that this incident could involve. There are lawyers, insurance agents, tire shops, auto dealers, physical therapists, chiropractors, urgent care, psychologists that all have an angle to educate about this story and that is to name just a few.

These local media companies, radios, and TVs, they're always looking for something to cover. If you are always putting out content and educating people then they're going to see you as the authority and want to contact you when there's some issue within the community or something that's relevant that people are talking about that you know the answers to. It's about being proactive and putting your message out there. If you don't get your message out there people aren't really going to be coming to you for information.

With many businesses being on the Internet now it's very easy for a person to just do a quick search and see that there might be six pest control companies all vying for the same pool of customers, and they're having trouble just trying to stand out. What makes them different from the competition?

When you do a search online you're going to come back with so many different options that it's really important for businesses to stand out from the competition. What we find with search now is that being #1 isn't what it used to be anymore, so if you're in the #1 position on Google, yes, you're still going to get a large portion of the traffic but they're not going to automatically do business with you. They're going to click on your website and have a look at your website, and they're immediately looking for those trust triggers. You have about 10 seconds to capture their attention, and if you can't do that within the first 10 seconds they're clicking off and they're going to the next one down the list.

It's extremely important that you stand out, and the thing I mentioned, those trust triggers that they see, those logos on your website, "Featured on ABC, NBC, CBS, CNN," that immediately captures their attention and they can stay on your site a little bit longer to find out more about your business. Again, you want to become that resource for information, so if you can answer their questions right there on your site you're going to be seen as that authority and a teacher, and you're going to make them want to pick up the phone and call you or come into your business. You really want to give as much information as you possibly can on your website as well as having those trust triggers there to immediately capture their attention.

This isn't about doing a hardcore sales pitch or writing sales letters. This is more about trying to be positioned to help your clients. People aren't coming to your website to read a sales letter. They're coming to your website to find solutions to problems, so if you can right away show that you solve problems, then people are more likely to do business with you.

Many of these local businesses, might need to really rework some of their existing website content to really highlight this idea of solving problems, being a problem solver, helping the clients so that they can get their problems fixed.

There's a lot of local businesses that needed a website, and they got somebody to create a website for them five, ten years ago that is still the same. It's never changed in the last five, ten years. They got a basic five-page website that has their basic pages but doesn't have any real information on it. People are going to click off those pages right away and they're going to somebody that looks like they can really solve their problem.

By doing that, when people see you as the educator and the advocate for their success, they're really going to search you out and they're going to choose you over the competition. That's how I think you stand out. They're going to trust you a lot more, and when it comes down to the actual sale it's going to be a little bit easier, the sales process, because you've shown that you are an advocate for their success. They do trust you, so the ease of sale is a lot better.

If they don't believe that you're the authority you have to work 10 times harder to get that customer and to keep that customer. If they do believe you're authority they're more willing to do business with you, and they're actually more willing to pay more money for the privilege of working with you, so it's really important to establish that authority before you do anything else.

Another thing local businesses can do to stand out is to be seen everywhere. Wherever your customers are hanging out, you need to be seen there. If they're doing a search on Google, you need to be seen there. If they're doing a search on Yelp, you need to be seen there. The more often you get seen the more trust they have that you are the main company in the market, and a great way, again, to do that is to repurpose that content. You might do an interview answering those 10 frequently asked question and the "should-ask" questions. You want to get that out across the board so no matter where people are online, where they're hanging out, whether it's on Facebook or Twitter or Instagram or YouTube, they're seeing you everywhere. You're branding and you're positioning yourself as the trusted authority by helping solve people's problems. You always have the answer.

The other thing that all that does is it helps you rank for those specific questions that people are typing in. Not a lot of business owners know this, but there's maybe five, ten, keywords that have the most searches in the marketplace. These local businesses are always trying to rank for those keywords and be seen for those keywords, which is great but that's only about 30% of the searches about their business and has the highest competition to get on the first page. The other 70% are those longer-tail keywords as we call them, and these are the real issues that people are having. Your prospects are typing in specific questions. If you really want to attract that 70% of the market you need to find out the questions they are asking and answer them. That way you get more traffic to your site and these searches are a lot easier to rank for as nobody else has taken the time to do this.

People are literally going to their Google search box and not typing in a keyword. They're typing in the entire question. To use the cleaning example again, people aren't just typing in "house cleaner"; they're typing in "non-toxic green cleaning company." If you can answer questions revolved around that kind of subject then you're going to show up first as the most relevant as opposed to some of these other companies that are just ranking for those house cleaning keywords.

Third-party recommendations are another way for people to stand out. Basically, it's what other people are saying about you, that is top of mind for people when they're searching for solutions to problems. They want to know what other peoples' experiences are, or they want some kind of testimonial, or review, or write-up to prove you are the authority. That's why it's so important to have ABC, NBC, CBS, FOX, those major channels, talking about you in a positive way because it goes so far in the mind of your prospects to set you up as the authority.

Talking about yourself, about you, and how long you've been in business, and what you offer, those aren't the things that people are really searching for. They're really looking for your authority and seeing if they're going to be able to trust you to give quality product or service for their hard-earned cash. It's all about the customer experience. They've got to believe that they're going to get a great customer experience, and that's what third-party recommendations do. It's all about having other people call you the expert and the authority rather than you trying to call yourself the expert.

Have Others Talk About You

Reviews and testimonials are extremely beneficial and extremely powerful as well, but you can also do spotlight articles where you're highlighted as an authority or an expert, and you're giving away valuable information. Again, coming back to that one problem, one solution, if you can do a specific article on that specific subject and have it appear on some of these major news channels, that gives you tremendous credibility that you are that educator, that advocate for the success of your customers. That's what draws people to you, gives you that trust and authority.

Write The Book

Writing a book also puts you way ahead of anybody else out there because nobody else is doing it. Nobody else is writing books on your specific industry, and to be able to walk into an office and see that the owner has written a book on the subject matter gives you tremendous credibility. There are two different levels of books. Writing a book and being a published author is something that, like I said, not many people do, but becoming a bestseller, that really makes you stand out from even all the other authors that may be out there, that have written something.

Instead of just standing out on a local level it can make you stand out on a national level, and when you've done that it really allows you to put yourself in a position to expand your business. We talked earlier about moving into other cities or counties. You can really expand when you've got a national bestseller. It really gives you that foundation of authority.

Having a book like that is the pinnacle of authority because people look at you differently, and they're a lot more willing to trust you. They're a lot more willing to give you more money for providing the service that you provide, so it gives you that instant credibility. First impressions for somebody that might not know you and comes into your business for the first time, if they see that you're a national bestseller they're going to be very confident, and trust that you're going to provide excellent service and their money's going to be well-spent giving it to you.

For local businesses that want to get even more exposure, are there other authority methods that they can explore. Authority marketing professionals call this the "authority wheel," with the center hub for all your content can be your blog or your business website. That's where you want to drive the traffic to because you want to drive traffic to your local business that has your main and your biggest message and has all you contact information on it. In order to drive that traffic you want to get it out on as many different places as possible. That's what we call "repurposing the content."

There's so many of these authority domains out there that Google loves to put on the first page, so by being part of that authority wheel you want to get on different things, like video, if you can get onto different video services like YouTube and Vimeo. Slideshare is another one that ranks really high in the search engines, that is basically just PowerPoint slides made into a video or just some information on slides that you share that ranks really high when people are looking for solutions.

Those authority media, like we talked about, each one of these can be a different spoke on the wheel, all driving traffic via links back to your main hub, being your business website or your blog. Social media, local directories, those are all online things. Then we have the offline for people who are walking into your office or if you're at events. You can be featured in magazines or have your book chapters out there. You wrote the books. You can put that out there for people to see.

The best way to do this stems from an audio interview. It might be a local radio station or you might just record it yourself: Have somebody ask you questions and you give the answers. You can get that information transcribed and you can put it out on all these different kinds of media. What that does is it drives the traffic back to you main business site, as well as having all those spokes in different places so people can find you and come back to your website.

Most people are familiar with: social media, blogging. A lot of people think of social media and blogging as personal things, like a personal journal or staying in contact with their family, but, a business should blog and be on social media in order to cultivate being seen as much as possible.

Familiarity provides trust to the marketplace, so if they're seeing you all the time it's like the branding that Coca-Cola does. You see their message all the time, so when you're thirsty you think, "Coke." If you've got a local business, you're a lawyer and you're giving information about certain things that happen, if you're say a divorce lawyer and you're giving information about the procedures for going through a divorce, or how to save your marriage, or what's going to happen with your children, or how much money you're going to have to pay out, if you can answer all these different questions then if you ever get into that situation where you need a lawyer, you're going to immediately think of that person and go to them because they're familiar to you.

That's why it's important to get the message out as many places as possible. If you can just go through and you can answer those 10 frequently asked questions and those 10 should-ask questions and get it out on all these different places, it's going to give you tons of material to share on social media. It's not you talking about yourself; it's you putting yourself in the position of being an educator and advocate for the success of your customers. You're really putting out a lot of goodwill in the marketplace by doing this, and like I said before, nobody is really doing this in you market, so if you just stand out a little bit more than your competition you're going to become that go-to person that everybody wants to do business with, and everybody talks about and talks about when they have the problems that you help solve.

In addition to online authority marketing tactics that a local business can use, there are still offline methods that can benefit from utilizing the authority model.

In local business marketing, face to face offline marketing efforts are still extremely powerful, especially if you are the front person of your business. If you are a doctor, a chiropractor, a lawyer, even the plumbers or landscapers, being the owner or the face of that business, you want to get out into the local community and share your message. Whether it's Meetups or BIN meetings or trade shows or any niche events, you really want to get out and share what you do.

When you're out there, and you're sharing, and you're talking to people, you want to share your authority. You don't necessarily want to talk about yourself all the time, but to hand somebody a magazine where you've been featured, or to hand somebody that's really interested in what you do, to hand them a book that you've been featured in or maybe a co-author of is extremely powerful. It's so much more powerful than trading business cards which get thrown away most of the time or just get piled up somewhere and forgotten.

People don't throw away books...ever, so if you want to be top of mind and you hand somebody a book it's a heck of a lot more powerful than just handing somebody a business card and be forgotten about.

Unfortunately, most local business owners are going to say, "What are you talking about, Neil? I can't write. How am I supposed to make a bestseller?"

This fear holds local business owners and entrepreneurs back from benefiting from a powerful way to establish their business as a leader in the field. Nobody is doing this right now, so to stand out and do this kind of thing is really going to establish you as the leader in your market. It doesn't take a great deal to write a book these days. You can talk to any business owner or leader about their specialized subject. They will be able to talk your ear off about what they know. They have all of that information in their head, and one of the best ways to do that is just to do an interview, like we talked about, and just maybe outline your book a little bit but then just talk about the certain things that you want to talk about and be able to talk all day about it.

Once you have that information on an MP3 or an audio file, you can get that transcribed and edited, and you can create that book very, very quickly, and fairly easily. Then it's about getting it out to the market, and creating that bestseller to give you the most bang for your buck and the greatest level of authority that you can. This could all be done in 60 to 90 days to get yourself a written book that is going to be with you for life, and get it to bestseller status.

Many business owners still think it takes a year to have a bestseller, but these days it's very, very quick. In fact, it can be done within that 60-, 90-day time frame. Some of the bestseller lists that people think of are The New York Times and the Wall Street Journal. Those are the two main ones that people think of, but there's also Amazon. Amazon is one of the biggest companies in the world and one of the most authoritative websites in the world, so to have a bestseller or Amazon just gives you the same amount of credibility. It's a lot easier to become a bestseller on Amazon than it is on Wall Street Journal or The New York Times, and the power of the positioning and the authority it brings is just the same.

For local businesses who see the value of establishing and positioning themselves as an authority, they want to know, "What does it take to become a local expert?"

First of all, like we said at the very beginning, you've got to establish your position and your message. Once that is clear to everybody, then we can move into building that foundation of authority, then developing a path and a plan for growth. You want to cement that message, and establish who you are in the community, and also to stay true to who you are. You don't want to dilute that message by trying to be something else, something that you don't want to do. You don't want to be everything to everyone because it dilutes your authority.

Think about if you wanted to go out for a good steak. Which one would you pick? Would you pick Fleming's Steakhouse or would you pick Golden Corral? I think everybody, if they had the money and they could afford it, they would pick Fleming's because they are the top-of-the-line steakhouse. I'm not too sure what the quality is when you go to Golden Corral for their steak because they do steak. They do chicken. They do pasta. They do Chinese. They do Mexican. They do Italian. They do a little bit of everything. It's kind of like that Jack of all trades and master of none.

You really want to establish that message and that positioning and stick to it. From there you want to build that solid foundation of authority and get that media attention right away. If you can get to that best-selling author status those two things alone are going to give you that solid foundation that everything else can be built on.

When you're building a house one of the most important things is to get your foundation right because if it's off just a little bit, everything that's built on top of that can run into problems and fail eventually, so when you're building that foundation of authority its really, really important to any business. Not many businesses start out that way. They start out by dipping the toe in the water, as you said, and seeing what they're good at and what bites without any actual plan. They're being told one way and being pulled another way by all the different sales calls that come in to them every day, so they're not really establishing that foundation for their business, which is a massive mistake.

As you probably know, 90% of businesses go out of business within the first five years, and one of the main reasons is that they haven't established themselves at all. They're still not sure after five years what it is that they do, so building that foundation of authority, like I've been saying, it can't ever be taken away from you once you have that bestselling author status. Once you've been featured on those media you can use those logos forever, and it's the best long-term return on investment that you can make in your business because all of your marketing efforts should be around your authority and positioning. It's going to increase your conversions and everything else for the life of your business. If nobody is doing this and if you can do that you build that solid foundation and you build a business that was built to last.

This is really about building your legacy and figuring out from the very beginning how big of a business that you want to have and what you want it to look like.

You have to have clear path and a plan when you're in business. Any business that isn't on a path is generally going to go nowhere. You've always got to have the goals that you're striving towards and know where you want to go. The first thing you need to do is decide what it is that you want to be. Then you can start with that foundation and figure out from there how you're going to get there. You have to have that clear path from that clear plan.

Once you've established that authority it's just continually getting that message of authority out there to your tribe, or your client, or people that do business with you so that you're always staying relevant. You're not a one-hit wonder. You've done something good once and then you're forgotten about. You always want to keep that authority and keep relevant in the market place. That's what helps you build a sustainable business, and a legacy, and puts you in a position of control and confidence when you really want to think about expanding your business.

If you're a doctor maybe you can bring in other doctors so that you can see more patients. If you're a lawyer maybe you can bring in new layers. Maybe you want to franchise if you're a cleaning company or a landscaping business. Once you have that solid foundation you can really start to think about building a business instead of just working your business, which is where the majority of business owners are. They're still working their business because they haven't built that foundation and they don't have a plan of where they want to go and who they want to be.

You can't really grow your business when you're working in your business. When you're working in your business you're constantly consumed with the demands of the business every day, solving people's problems. Maybe some really enjoy doing it, which is great but it's not really going to expand your business any further. Any business that is really going to grow eventually has to come to a point where you have to be the marketer of your business rather than the doer of your business.

You can find people, generally, to do what you do. You can find other educated people, whether they're doctors, lawyers, chiropractors, or you can find somebody to sit in and do your job while you go about expanding your business. Ways that you can do that, speaking of the publicity, is to get out there and be on radio, and to make yourself available at meetings and to lead groups. That's the way that you really establish yourself as a celebrity in your marketplace, and that celebrity authority position is the most attractive to money. It's going to just draw people to you even more, in a greater way than if you were just still at your business doing your business.

You have to be able to break away from your business and position yourself as that authority, and be seen in the public, and always be available for publicity if you're ever really going to grow your business to any real substantial business that can be left as a legacy.

This makes me think of the sharks on the television show Shark Tank. They've got that coveted celebrity authority status. They all are obviously entrepreneurs and business people but now, because of the show, they have all of this publicity and media attention, and really because they are the celebrity and an authority at each of their individual industries they get all kinds of deals without really having to try, versus someone who doesn't have that attention with that celebrity status.

If you're the celebrity in your local market, it can be as powerful as celebrity in a national sense for your business. It may be that you're the well-known dentist in your area. You're the well-known doctor in your area. Everybody knows your name.

The Shark Tank effect has really launched businesses out there, and it's not necessarily ... Even the businesses that don't get deals are still launched just by being on that program. You find a lot of the business owners go on specifically to get that strategic partnership, which is basically doing the same thing that these authority media sites are doing for local businesses. They're just lending that authority that these sharks have built over their careers. It's lending that authority to them. That's the whole purpose of people going on that show is to get that authority and that third party credibility from working with one of the sharks, but it is the same principal in the local market.

Obviously not every business can go on the Shark Tank and have that short amount of time to get their viewers and get that launch, but using authority marketing and authority positioning is a way that other types of businesses can essentially do the same thing. It doesn't take as long as most people believe to become a local authority. You can become a bestseller in 60 to 90 days. Being featured on the media is a very quick process as well. It really doesn't take that long to become a local authority. Remember, all of this can be manufactured.

We're not waiting for people to anoint us as the authority. We're proactively going out. We're finding our positioning and we're using that positioning and letting everybody know that we've been positioned as an authority. Some of our clients, by being positioned on ABC and NBC and CBS and having articles done about them and their business, just a simple post to Facebook has completely changed their business. People are liking and commenting on it and saying, "Oh my goodness, this is so great. I'm so proud of you."

All of a sudden they're looked at in a different way than they may have been before. Something as simple as a Facebook post sharing that you've been positioned as an expert and authority is enough to completely change the life of a business from that point on. It's all about getting that continued content out there so that you're staying relevant, but being positioned as a local authority can be extremely quick.

Anybody can go into a market and, with the right tools, can stand out as the authority and take over because we're using this positioning, but you have to have some substance if you're going to last. If I wanted to go into the real estate market here in Atlanta I could do all the things that I need to do to position myself as the best, and I would draw people to me, but if I didn't know how to write a contract, or close the deal, or I didn't know the answers to the questions I'm not going to last very long,

Anybody can come into the market and position themselves as the authority, but you have to be able to back that up, and that's what the manufactured celebrity is. They're just using the tools that are available to us, like the Amazon bestseller and the book deals, positioning yourself on radio and those other kinds of things to get your message out there. That doesn't take a great deal of effort. Anybody, really, can do it. It's just that most people won't or they don't know about it.

You look, again, at Paris Hilton or the Kardashians or Bruce or Caitlyn, whatever he or she is going by, Jenner these days. They don't really have a great deal of substance. Who are they? What have they done? All they've done is they've used the media and the power of the media to put themselves in a position of always being talked about. It shows you how powerful the media is if you really just know how to use it. They've all made millions of dollars off their position of celebrity in the media, and they don't really have any talents to speak of, but because they're always in the spotlight they're in that position of authority and they're able to attract people to them. They're using it to make a living, just being in the spotlight.

You look at somebody else that's always in the spotlight, Donald Trump, especially with his presidential candidacy right now. He has made his name in the real estate and the business markets, and he has positioned himself as the celebrity, the ultimate, the celebrity authority. He's always relevant, and he commands crazy figures. I just saw some statistics the other day in Washington, D.C., their political spectrum, and what they charge for their speeches. Donald Trump, for a 90-minute speech commands $1.5 million dollars for a 90-minute speech.

Is Donald Trump the best speaker in the world, that he can command that exorbitant price? No, he's just a positioned himself as the celebrity authority, and he's able to ask for that price and people will pay it. The next person down the list, the next highest person was $400,000. There's a huge difference between Donald Trump and the next person on the list. I think Hilary Clinton was somewhere around there, but she was nowhere near. She was about $200,000. It just shows you what that position of authority can really do for you. Donald Trump is also overwhelmingly dominating the social media channels and is now up there in the poles where nobody gave him a chance when he first entered the race.

There are certain things you can do to always be in the spotlight when it comes to your market. You don't have to be nationally famous, you just need to be famous to that local market that is most important to you.

First, you need to establish a strong foundation, a firm platform. The best way to do that is to be featured in your local and national media, and that would be the first step so that you can use those logos, and put them on your website as trust triggers, so when people go to you, immediately they're going to have that trust in you because you've been featured as an authority.

The next thing is to publish a book, whether it's a book chapter, you could be a co-contributor, to a book in your market or just as a business leader, but to become a published author is extremely important, as well as becoming that bestselling author, which is the pinnacle. Once you have that established you really have something to build your business on, and that's the blueprint for success. Like I said, this can be done in 60 to 90 days because all business owners and leaders have all the expert knowledge inside their head. It's just a case of getting it out through an interview and getting it on paper so it can be transferred into a book, so it can be very quick.

Once you have this media attention, it is important to keep staying in the spotlight. You never want to be forgotten. You always want to stay in the spotlight. One of the ways that you can do that is by putting out new content or repurposing content that's already been out there. Maybe once you put an article from ABC on your social media, maybe the next week you put something out on YouTube. It's always about putting something out where you've been featured as the authority and always being relevant.

Another great way to be relevant in different markets is to align with different JV partners, which is joint venture. Maybe you can find somebody that has something in common with your business. Get with them and share your expertise with them. For an example, two completely unrelated markets, I talked about my wife with the cleaning business. Another market that needs cleaning businesses is real estate, so if you can partner up with a couple of strategic real estate companies they can give you hundreds of jobs a year, which can really transform your business.

Aligning with different partners is very important. It's not something that people think about all the time, going outside of their industry and trying to align with somebody else. It can be extremely beneficial. Another way to do that is by aligning with different charities, and there are massive amounts of influential people that are involved in these charities. If you can get even a sponsor of some events you get people talking about you. You're making very important connections in that community.

It's all about getting your authority out there and being able to get out and talk to people, and meet the people, and develop those relationships, and charities, and different causes, and clubs, and strategic partnerships, are a great way to do that on a big scale rather than just getting it out within your own little market.

CHAPTER SEVEN

Local business owners see and understand the value of establishing themselves as an authority and positioning their company, but they have hard questions such as, "What's my return on investment going to be for authority marketing?"

What's the ROI On Authority?

You can't really put a price on the benefit of authority marketing and building this foundation because it's going last a lifetime, so it's very hard to quantify it. We talk about macroeconomics, which is the big picture. It's not just one single thing that you're doing for your business. It's not like buying pay-per-click traffic. You spend $1,000 in pay-per-click traffic and you get a certain amount of business. That's your $1,000 gone. You got that business and it's over. With the authority marketing, what it does is it increases your brand. It increases your conversions, and all those things are measured over a lifetime. It's the same across the board in all your marketing.

A phrase in the financial market is "a rising tide lifts all boats." That's kind of what it's like with authority marketing. No matter what kind of marketing and advertising you do it's going to benefit from you having this authority positioning. Whether it's online marketing of offline marketing, by being positioned as the authority is going to help you close way more deals than not having it.

Specifically, I did this with our own cleaning company. We were spending about $300 a week on advertising. It's still a fairly small family-run business but we were spending $300 a week on pay-per-click advertising to get the specific return. As soon as we put the authority on our website, and this was just a banner that said, "Featured on ABC, NBC, CBS, and FOX," that was the only change that we made as well as on our pay-per-click ads said "featured on ABC, CBS, NBS, and FOX," so when people are searching us out we're getting more clicks than we were before.

The way pay-per-click works is the more clicks you get, the higher your click-through rate, the less that Google actually charges you. What happened was we immediately started ... We saved 40% on our advertising costs as well as saving 40% of that $300 that we're spending every week. We also increased all our prices and we had no drop in sales, so if you can measure all that kind of return on investment then you're going to come out with a grand, grand number. This can all be measured over a lifetime as well, so it is the greatest investment you can make in your business. Period.

Our other customers and clients have had the same kind of experience with just once they've been positioned properly the business takes on a whole new life. Another important point, and this is where you can really think about growing your business too, is if you can spend the money you are saving on advertising costs back into your business, you can make a real difference. If I have to reinvest that $300 or the 40% that I was saving, I reinvest it into getting more customers, I would grow my business really, really quickly. Before the authority positioning in the cleaning business the average customer acquisition cost was right around $50. So, with $300 that was buying 6 new customers at an average of $165 for the first job. So that is $990 return for a $300 investment. After authority positioning the average customer acquisition cost was around $30. So, $300 invested bought 10 new customers with an average sale of $185. That's $1850 for a $300 ad spend. That's almost double the business for the same amount of advertising. Now, they are great results and all businesses are different, but what would an increase of 10% do for your business? How about 50%, or even 100%. It is all possible once you are positioned correctly in your local market.

A key to really dominate and control your market is, whoever can afford to spend the most to acquire a customer wins. If I can spend more than my competition to get a customer by putting out more and more ads and driving more and more business to my company then eventually I'm going to dominate and I'm going to take over that market.

So, in the example above, if I took the extra $860 a week that I was making as well as my original $300 and invested into advertising, I would be spending $1160 a week in marketing and gaining 38 new customers a week generating $7030 in business for a $5870 profit. At $50 per customer my competition would have to spend $1900 for 38 new customers generating $6270 in business for a $4370 profit.

This is all exponential too. If you have the people in place of course to provide the proper quality service, you can see how quickly you can grow and dominate. So, there are some return on investment numbers to think about.

Obviously, these numbers are just as an example and hypothetical. There are a lot of other factors to think about that may stop a local business growing this fast like having the qualified people to deliver your service. It just goes to show that the results are possible once you have that positioning to dominate.

This is not a one-time thing, like the pay-per-click, where when your money is used up it's used up. This is an everlasting investment. In my own business, one of the first results that I saw is that the resistance to sales was a lot less. We initially had people haggling over price: "What's your price for this." "It's $150." "Oh, I don't want to pay that much. Can you do it for $80?" Since we put that positioning of authority on our site we don't have those conversations anymore. It's $159. If you don't want to pay it you don't want to pay it. We have plenty more people coming in, so with that lifetime results it's always attracting new customers to your business as well.

It's attracting people all the time, so you don't have to just take anything that's out there. You can pick and choose which jobs that you want to take, and pick and choose also how fast you want to grow. It also gives you more qualified customers, clients, or patients. People who see your site and want to do business with you understand that they're going to have to pay a little bit more. They understand that they're going to get quality and they're willing to pay more for that quality.

With all the logos and everything, that increases the effectiveness of all media, whether it's online or offline. It might be a radio advertisement. It might be TV exposure. It might be direct mail. Dentists do a lot of direct mail to try and get that local area. If you can show that you've been featured on ABC, NBC, CBS, FOX, bestselling author, that's going to give you credibility and increase the conversions and the effectiveness of that piece of advertising. That solid foundation really works over all different forms of media.

When you're talking about strategic partners as well it makes it easier to work with those people, and it makes your business easier to recommend because of your positioning. That return on investment is very hard to quantify, but it lasts a lifetime. The conversions alone are where you see the biggest return on invest instantly, but it's so much deeper than that. There are so many different things that you don't really see that factor into you growing that business and profit long term.

Business owners should look at the bigger picture when calculating their ROI, the macroeconomics of authority marketing." There are things that we might not automatically think of that should be taken into account in the return on investment.

The overall branding of being positioned like that, you're branding yourself as an authority from that day forward, that you have your book or your media exposure. That branding is sustainable over a lifetime. Just that branding alone is going to bring more qualified people to your business. If they're doing a search online and they click on your site, maybe eight out of ten people would normally click off and go and find somebody else, but because you've got that branding on your site, that authority, it means more people are staying on your site and doing business with you.

Branding is extremely important. It's not the big-box branding that we're talking about. It's more direct response, and you have to have that balance between branding and direct response. The branding is good, and giving the content, and answers the questions, and everything is wonderful, but you still have to have your message that goes out to people that says, "Come to my business," and give them an actual call to action to bring them in. That balance is important, but branding is very important within your local market, your local niche, so we're not talking about spending tons of money on that big-box branding like Coca-Cola or Nike.

The bottom line is, there are two major ways that you can increase profits. You can either sell more stuff or you can increase you price. In order to sell more stuff you have to work a lot harder, and it takes up more of your time and more of your resource, but certainly you can increase your profits if you're selling more stuff. If all things remained the same, if you just doubled your prices you'd pretty much double your business instantly. That's what the power of authority can do for your business. It gives you the positioning and the platform where you can raise your prices and still get the same amount of customers if not more because people really want to work with people in the position of authority.

If you can raise your prices, it might not be doubling your prices, but if you can increase even 10%, what would that do to any local business to increase 10% year over year? It would make a substantial difference to any business. People expect to pay you more due to your position in the marketplace. I mentioned a little bit before, only about 10% of buying decisions are actually based on price, so really what you need to be working on is establishing that positioning and trust, which is the major part of buying decisions, that people feel like you're a good fit for them.

Price is where 90% of businesses get hung up on, and they try and compete over price, but it's only really 10% of the buying decision. The fastest way, really, to increase your profits is to increase your price. There's three things that you really need to increase profits, and that's positioning, promotion, and then the process. The great thing is that 90% of the people out there are working on the process, and that means doing different kinds of advertising, maybe advertising a sale on this, or a sale on that, or if you're online, maybe changing your shopping cart or the font here, or changing something up in your store.

Now, that's all the process, which can help the ease of sale, but it's not the most effective place to start, at least initially. The most effective place to start, to increase those profits as quick as possible is on your positioning. That's why it's so powerful, and really nobody in your market is doing it, so you're going to be light years ahead if you take your stance and you work on your positioning.

Positioning is really about increasing your value to your client. The more value you have in your marketplace the more you're going to get paid. There's the value of your equation as well. You've got two different kinds of value. You've got practical value and then you've got intrinsic value. The more intrinsic value than you can get the more total perceived value you're going to have. Let me give you an example. In the luxury motor industry you've got a BMW 750, which is a very nice car. It's priced at just under $100,000. Then you've got a Rolls-Royce Ghost, which just the name "Rolls-Royce" alone is going to tell you it's positioned as the best and it's going to cost more. This guy comes in at about $300,000.

We've got two cars here. One's $100,000 and the other is $300,000. They're both in the luxury sphere, but what makes one 300% better than the other? Look at the practical value of the car. What's the practical value? You can ride along in it. You can travel faster than you can walking. You're able to put your stuff in it. You can put your family in it. It's going to keep you dry if it rains. Those are all practical things about the car.

For the BMW, inside maybe it's very well appointed. It's got nice leather. It's dependable. It rides well. It looks cool. Those are all practical things, but the same can be said of the Rolls Royce. It has the same practical value as the BMW. What makes it 300% more expensive than the BMW? When you consider BMW actually owns Rolls-Royce, the company, and the chassis of the car is basically the same. The Rolls-Royce is built on the BMW chassis, so the cars, from a practical standpoint, aren't that different. The big difference here is the intrinsic value.

The intrinsic value of the Rolls-Royce Ghost is what people think about you when you're driving up in a Rolls-Royce because the Rolls-Royce has been positioned as the best of the best. Only the best of the best are able to afford to buy a Rolls-Royce, and only the best of the best drive a Rolls-Royce, so what you're paying for basically is that kind of positioning. The more of that you can get in your business the more value you're going to have.

You imagine somebody to drive up to a meeting in a Rolls-Royce Ghost. That person is going to immediately be positioned as an authority, as a leader, as successful, and people are going to want to know more about that person, do business with that person. Basically that's what intrinsic value is, and that's what people are paying for. They're paying for that value that you build largely through positioning.

If you think about computers: the iPhones, the Mac computers are considered the best, and when they come out with a new model people are standing in line to buy these phones, $600, $700. Buy the computers for the thousands of dollars. They never give discounts on any of their products and, like I said, a new model comes out which is pretty much similar to the last model that came out six months ago, but still people are clamoring over each other to buy that product.

It's the same with Ferrari as well. A new Ferrari comes out. The dealership doesn't have to do anything to sell this new model there's actually a waiting list to buy the car. They're going to say, "Okay, it's $300,000 for this Ferrari," but if you want it they're going to add another $50,000 to $60,000 on top just to get to the top of the pecking over. When you have that authority in the positioning the ease of the sales process becomes super easy. You don't have to convince anybody to do business with you or to buy your stuff. That authority does it all for you, and it's all brought about by positioning yourself as the Rolls-Royce of your industry basically.

What businesses need to do to really put into practice this idea of increasing their value (not just the practical value, but the intrinsic value and the perceived value of their brand as well) they need to pay attention to authority positioning.

The Authority Ladder

Think of authority positioning like a ladder, the authority ladder. You basically get paid for your position in the marketplace, so the authority ladder goes from a generalist. When you think about a generalist you talk about the medical field. A generalist might be like a general practitioner. They're going to get paid the least in the marketplace, in the medical field. A step up from that would be a specialist. The specialist might be a heart surgeon. They're going to get paid a lot more than the generalist. Then a step up from that would be an authority.

An authority might be who the other heart surgeons in your local area, if there's something they're not too sure or comfortable with, they might recommend you to another heart surgeon, so that would be the authority. Then from there we go on to talk about the celebrity, which might be a well-known heart surgeon throughout the country, and then the ultimate position on the authority ladder is the celebrity authority. That, like I said before, is the most attractive to money. People like Dr. Phil and Dr. Oz, they might not be the biggest or the best at what they do but because they've been positioned as the authority and they're the celebrity authority, you'll find that they get the most money than the other doctors out there.

Being positioned as that celebrity authority is the ultimate. We've talked about Donald Trump charging $1.5 million for a 90-minute speech. We've talked about Dave Ramsey and Suze Orman and Jim Cramer. These are like the celebrity authorities in their own market. We've talked about the Shark Tank effect, and just being associated with the sharks is enough to build businesses for a lifetime with those strategic partners.

The higher up that ladder you go the more people that you're going to attract and the more money you're going to be able to charge because people want to do business with authority, so authorities rule, and people are magnetically attracted to authorities. There's never any shortage of work for people who are at the top. If you're the best-know plastic surgeon in the country people are going to fly from all over the world to do business with you. If you can position yourself and make yourself go up that ladder, the further up that ladder you go the more successful you're going to be.

People are always attracted to the businesses who are at the top, and that goes from the local market all the way up to national and international level. You want to stay relevant, always putting out new content, making sure that people know that you're the expert. People that want to do business with you, you always want to be educating your tribe. Always give them the content so you're always top of mind. When somebody is looking to solve a problem that you solve they're going to think of you first.

We talked about staying up to date with new technology but incorporating those old-school values because ultimately we do business with people. We don't do business with websites. We do business with people and people want to have that relationship, so it's extremely important that we involve great customer service and goodwill in what we do.

People want to be respected and treated well, and they'll pay for that. People are very disenfranchised with business and the market as a whole. They find it very hard to trust anybody these days, so anybody whose theme is an advocate for the customer's success is really going to attract people to them. We do business with people and we need to establish good relationships. We want to be respected, so when we share that through social media, and not necessarily talking about our own expertise all the time, but sharing how you've helped different people succeed and get their desired outcome, that's what people want. They want to belong to people like you and a company like you.

Chick-fil-A springs to mind in the fast food industry. They have great customer service and people want to go back there because of the customer service. We go there two, three times a week probably, and it's not because of they're the cheapest place in town. It's because we feel welcome when we go in there, and people are very nice to you. They put extra staff out just to develop that customer experience. That's extremely important and people want that experience. They crave it and they don't mind paying for it.

Creating goodwill within the market is extremely important. It develops customers for life. They become loyal to you. It increases the longevity, the lifetime value of a customer, and of course it gets people talking about you, giving referrals, which is a great foundation. That's free advertising, basically, for your business. An example is Apple. One of the little slogans about Apple is, "Once you go Mac, you never go back." Once you've had an Apple computer, you deal with the customer service and everything, you never go back to a PC just because the experience is so much greater. It's really important from that perspective to develop a relationship with your customers and to stand out as the authority when you're doing that.

To dominate their target market, a local business needs to establish themselves as an authority. In this way, you build trust, and that is one of the most important things in today's market. If you build your marketing on trust you're going to be a lot more successful if you just build it around your expertise. Eighty percent of sales are based on liking and trusting the salesperson, so it's extremely important to have trust at the center of your market.

Also, a third of people believe that most people can't be trusted. That doesn't do well for most people who are trying to be salesy and push products on you, because if you come at them from that perspective, if a third of people think that most people can't be trusted then that's not a great place to start. Dan Kennedy is a great marketer and mentor, talks about the 9 gates to customer commitment. You really need to be answering a lot of the questions that are in the minds of your prospects.

By positioning yourself as an authority is it's going to immediately answer a lot of these questions, questions like, "Is this guy for real?" That is authenticity. "Is he telling me the truth?" Believability. "Is he knowledgeable and competent?" which is authority. "Is he appropriate for me?" which is feasibility of the relationship. "Is he listening or just peddling?" which is personability. "Overall, can he be relied on?" which is trustability. "Do I understand enough what he's going to do for me?" which is comfort. "Am I making the best choice versus other choices?" which is superiority. "Am I paying a fair price?" which is value.

Those are the 9 gates to customer commitment Dan Kennedy talks about. As you can see, a lot of these are answered by positing yourself as an authority. Local and national media companies are going to be covering people who are authentic. They put you in a position of believability and trustworthiness. They put you into a position of authority and superiority, and then, like I said, only 10% of most sales come down to the actual price, but 80% come down to likely and trusting the salesperson. This is what most businesses should be focusing on, but most people still are still worried about the price that they're charging.

Referral business has been business before the Internet was around, and still people talk through social media now, or whether it's still face to face. That's why these sites like Angie's List and HomeAdvisor and these other things are very popular. It's because people are looking for referrals or reviews from other people who have had experience with that same business, but like we said at the start, people are on the Internet all the time, so when they get a referral from somebody, they're going to the internet to check out to establish that this company is for real. Even though they got a personal recommendation they're still going to the Internet to check out this company.

If you have a bad website or you don't have much of a presence they're still going to be a little bit wary of it, but when you have that good solid presence and you got a great referral they're almost guaranteed to get that business. Reviews and testimonials and some of those third-party authority sites are really important. In fact, Neilson did a study back in 2012 about what was the most authoritative kind of referral that people get, and the personal referral was the best, at 90%. The second was online reviews, which was 72%.

Back then in 2012, 72% of people trusted online reviews almost as much as a personal recommendation, but since that they've done another one in 2015, and that 72% has gone up to 88%, which means people are trusting the online reviews just as much as a personal recommendation from a friend or a family member. To get these online reviews and this third-party recommendation from trusted authorities is extremely important.

CONCLUSION

We've talked about a lot of different ways that local businesses can use authority positioning and authority marketing tactics to put themselves in a better position to get their ideal clients. The winning formula is whoever can pay the most to acquire a customer wins.

If you can spend more money on advertising, then you're going to get more customers to your business. The way you do that is by establishing yourself as the authority in your market. That's going to allow you to increase your prices. It's going to allow you to spend more money on advertising. It's going to allow you to save money because you're having increased conversions.

Whether it's on pay per click, SEO, direct mail, you're going to get more customers. Because you're creating more goodwill in the marketplace you're going to get more referrals, which is free advertising, and it's all based around that foundation of authority.

The first place for any business is to establish themselves as the authority in the marketplace by doing those things that we've talked about: writing a book, which can be very easy because all the knowledge is in their head, getting some quality information on those media outlets like ABC, NBC, CBS.

What that does is it creates that platform that gives you that authority forever, so it helps you build that legacy. You establish your authority and you've got that blueprint for success that can be built upon.

You can now think about expanding by opening new stores or offices or clinics. You can take on additional clients. You can franchise.

It really puts you in a position of control to build a business knowing that you have that foundation to rely on, and that you're not going to go anywhere anytime soon. It's the #1 thing, by establishing your authority, the #1 thing that you can do to exponentially increase you leads, your customers, your sales, and your profits, and it's the fastest thing that any business can do to change their business and to change their life.

For those interested in learning more about how to best position their local business as an authority and expert in their field, the best way to get a hold of me is through my website, which is http://www.theauthorityarchitect.com. People can go there and receive additional information from me, I'll send it to their doorstep, a little bit more in depth about authority positioning, and how they can get started.

ABOUT THE AUTHOR

Neil Howe is an online media strategist who works with business owners to create a platform of authority for their marketing and advertising. He is a best-selling author, contributor to CNN, USA Today as well as Small Business Trendsetters and Business Innovators Magazine. Neil has been working to help businesses build a solid foundation of authority and give them the platform they need to explode their business in ever more competitive markets.

He delivers an eye-opening look at the core of all business – positioning and authority, and teaches you the secrets to acquiring it, keeping it and using it to build a stand out business, increase your prices, and attract more high paying clients that generate referrals. You'll get the time-tested strategies required to build trust and goodwill in an understandably skeptical world, and in turn, attract more business and profits while creating a legacy for your family.

Neil Howe is "The Authority Architect." He is the founder of A.C.E. Marketing based in Atlanta, Georgia. He can be reached online at: www.theauthorityarchitect.com.

www.ingramcontent.com/pod-product-compliance
Lightning Source LLC
Chambersburg PA
CBHW060627210326
41520CB00010B/1502